MW00331045

Presented To:

_____

Given By:

_____

On the Date Of:

_____

*As iron sharpens iron,
a friend sharpens a friend.*

—

Proverbs 27:17 NLT

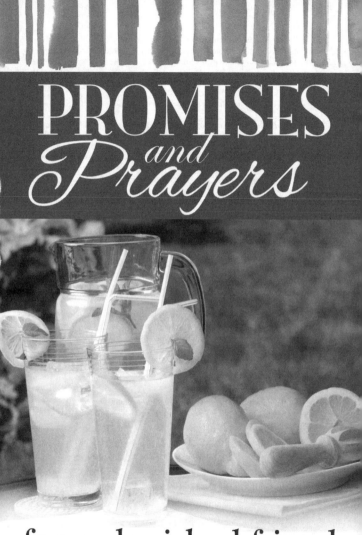

PROMISES
and
Prayers

for a cherished friend

The quoted ideas expressed in this book (but not Scripture verses) are not, in all cases, exact quotations, as some have been edited for clarity and brevity. In all cases, the author has attempted to maintain the speaker's original intent. In some cases, quoted material for this book was obtained from secondary sources, primarily print media. While every effort was made to ensure the accuracy of these sources, the accuracy cannot be guaranteed. For additions, deletions, corrections, or clarifications in future editions of this text, please write Freeman-Smith.

The Holy Bible, King James Version

The Holy Bible, New King James Version (NKJV) Copyright © 1982 by Thomas Nelson, Inc. Used by permission.

New century Version®. (NCV) Copyright © 1987, 1988, 1991 by Word Publishing, a division of Thomas Nelson, Inc. All rights reserved. Used by permission.

The Holman Christian Standard Bible™ (HCSB) Copyright © 1999, 2000, 2001 by Holman Bible Publishers. Used by permission.

The Holy Bible, New International Version®. (NIV) Copyright © 1973, 1978, 1984 International Bible Society. Used by permission of Zondervan. All rights reserved.

The Holy Bible. New Living Translation (NLT) copyright © 1996 Tyndale Charitable Trust. Used by permission of Tyndale House Publishers.

The New American Standard Bible®, (NASB) Copyright © 1960, 1962, 1963, 1968, 1971, 1972, 1973, 1975, 1977, 1995 by The Lockman Foundation. Used by permission.

Scripture taken from The Message. (MSG) Copyright © 1993, 1994, 1995, 1996, 2000, 2001, 2002. Used by permission of NavPress Publishing Group.

Cover Design by Kim Russell / Wahoo Designs
Page Layout by Bart Dawson

ISBN 978-1-60587-431-9

Printed in the United States of America

1 2 3 4 5—CHG—16 15 14 13 12

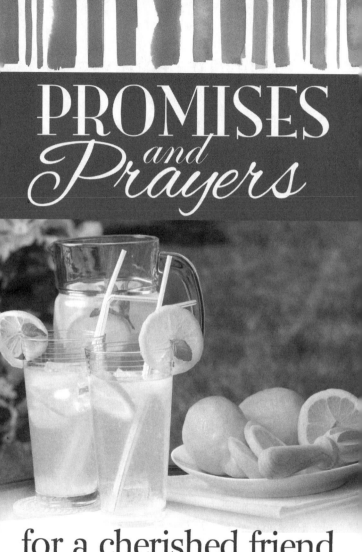

PROMISES *and* *Prayers*

for a cherished friend

TABLE OF CONTENTS

INTRODUCTION

L oyal Christian friendship is ordained by God. Throughout the Bible, we are reminded to love one another, to care for one another, and to treat one another as we wish to be treated. This collection of devotional readings is a celebration of Christian friendship. As such, it is intended to help you, the reader, in your efforts to be the kind of friend that God intends.

Perhaps you received this book as a gift from a trusted companion, or perhaps you picked it up on your own. Either way, you will be blessed if you take the words of these pages to heart.

This text addresses 30 topics. Each brief chapter contains Bible verses, a brief devotional reading, quotations from noted Christian thinkers, and a prayer. The ideas in each chapter are powerful reminders of God's commandments and of the joys of Christian friendship.

Because you have taken time to open this book and begin reading it, you understand the important role that Christian friendship plays in God's plans for His kingdom and for your life. Christ promises His followers a life of abundance (John 10:10). May your friends bless you abundantly, and may you do the same for them.

THE JOYS OF FRIENDSHIP

Beloved, if God so loved us,
we also ought to love one another.

—

1 John 4:11 NKJV

W hat is a friend? The dictionary defines the word friend as "a person who is attached to another by feelings of affection or personal regard." This definition is accurate, as far as it goes, but when we examine the deeper meaning of friendship, so many more descriptors come to mind: trustworthiness, loyalty, helpfulness, kindness, understanding, forgiveness, encouragement, humor, and cheerfulness, to mention but a few.

Genuine friendship should be treasured, protected, and nourished. And how do we do so? By observing the Golden Rule: As Christians, we are commanded to treat others as we wish to be treated (Matthew 7:12). When we treat others with kindness, courtesy, and respect, we build friendships that can last a lifetime. And God smiles.

Do you want to have trustworthy, encouraging friends? Then be one. And make no mistake: that's exactly the kind of friend that God wants you to be.

Wisdom from God's Holy Word

A friend loves at all times, and a brother is born for a difficult time.

Proverbs 17:17 HCSB

Iron sharpens iron, and one man sharpens another.

Proverbs 27:17 HCSB

Finally, all of you be of one mind, having compassion for one another; love as brothers, be tenderhearted, be courteous.

1 Peter 3:8 NKJV

The one who loves his brother remains in the light, and there is no cause for stumbling in him.

1 John 2:10 HCSB

No one has greater love than this, that someone would lay down his life for his friends.

John 15:13 HCSB

More Great Ideas

Friendship is the greatest of worldly goods. Certainly to me it is the chief happiness of life. If I had to give a piece of advice to a young man about a place to live, I think I should say, "sacrifice almost everything to live where you can be near your friends." I know I am very fortunate in that respect.

C. S. Lewis

We long to find someone who has been where we've been, who shares our fragile skies, who sees our sunsets with the same shades of blue.

Beth Moore

Inasmuch as anyone pushes you nearer to God, he or she is your friend.

Barbara Johnson

You could have been born in another time and another place, but God determined to "people" your life with these particular friends.

Joni Eareckson Tada

Don't bypass the potential for
meaningful friendships
just because of differences.
Explore them. Embrace them.
Love them.

—

Luci Swindoll

Today's Timely Tip

Remember that the friends you choose can make a profound impact on every other aspect of your life. So choose carefully and prayerfully.

Today's Prayer

Thank You, Lord, for the Friend I have in Jesus. And, thank You for the dear friends You have given me, the friends who enrich my life. I pray for them today, and ask Your blessings upon them. Amen

PRAYING FOR OUR FRIENDS

Be kindly affectionate to one another with brotherly love, in honor giving preference to one another; not lagging in diligence, fervent in spirit, serving the Lord; rejoicing in hope, patient in tribulation, continuing steadfastly in prayer.

—

Romans 12:10–12 NKJV

J esus made it clear to His disciples: they should pray always. And so should we. Genuine, heartfelt prayer changes things and it changes us. When we lift our hearts to our Father in heaven, we open ourselves to a never-ending source of divine wisdom, limitless power, and infinite love.

Today, we offer a prayer of thanks to God for our friends. Loyal Christian friends have much to offer us: encouragement, faith, fellowship, and fun, for starters. And when we align ourselves with godly believers, we are blessed by them and by our Creator.

Let us thank God for all the people who love us—for the family and friends whom He has placed along our paths. And let's pray for our family and friends with sincere hearts. God hears our prayers, and He responds.

Wisdom from God's Holy Word

And everything—whatever you ask in prayer, believing—you will receive.

Matthew 21:22 HCSB

Rejoice always! Pray constantly. Give thanks in everything, for this is God's will for you in Christ Jesus.

1 Thessalonians 5:16-18 HCSB

Therefore I want the men in every place to pray, lifting up holy hands without anger or argument.

1 Timothy 2:8 HCSB

The intense prayer of the righteous is very powerful.

James 5:16 HCSB

Yet He often withdrew to deserted places and prayed.

Luke 5:16 HCSB

More Great Ideas

Your family and friends need your prayers and you need theirs. And God wants to hear those prayers. So what are you waiting for?

Marie T. Freeman

There is no way that Christians, in a private capacity, can do so much to promote the work of God and advance the kingdom of Christ as by prayer.

Jonathan Edwards

Prayer is never the least we can do; it is always the most!

A. W. Tozer

A life growing in its purity and devotion will be a more prayerful life.

E. M. Bounds

Prayer guards hearts and minds and causes God to bring peace out of chaos.

Beth Moore

We can do nothing
without prayer.
All things can be done by
importunate prayer.
That is the teaching of
Jesus Christ.

—

E. M. Bounds

Today's Timely Tip

Prayer changes things—and you—so pray.

Today's Prayer

Dear Lord, make me a person whose constant prayers are pleasing to You. Let me come to You often with concerns both great and small. I trust in the power of prayer, Father, because prayer changes things and it changes me. In the quiet moments of the day, I will open my heart to You. I know that You are with me always and that You always hear my prayers. So I will pray and be thankful. Amen

DAY 3

TRUSTING GOD'S PROMISES

*All Scripture is inspired by God and is
profitable for teaching, for rebuking,
for correcting, for training in righteousness,
so that the man of God may be complete,
equipped for every good work.*

—

2 Timothy 3:16-17 HCSB

God's promises are found in a book like no other: the Holy Bible. The Bible is a roadmap for life here on earth and for life eternal. As Christians, we are called upon to trust its promises, to follow its commandments, and to share its Good News.

As believers, we must study the Bible daily and meditate upon its meaning for our lives. Otherwise, we deprive ourselves of a priceless gift from our Creator. God's Holy Word is, indeed, a transforming, life-changing, one-of-a-kind treasure. And, a passing acquaintance with the Good Book is insufficient for Christians who seek to obey God's Word and to understand His will.

God has made promises to mankind and to you. God's promises never fail and they never grow old. You must trust those promises and share them with your family, with your friends, and with the world.

Wisdom from God's Holy Word

Man shall not live by bread alone, but by every word that proceeds from the mouth of God.

Matthew 4:4 NKJV

For I am not ashamed of the gospel, because it is God's power for salvation to everyone who believes.

Romans 1:16 HCSB

Heaven and earth will pass away, but My words will never pass away.

Matthew 24:35 HCSB

For the word of God is living and effective and sharper than any two-edged sword, penetrating as far as to divide soul, spirit, joints, and marrow; it is a judge of the ideas and thoughts of the heart.

Hebrews 4:12 HCSB

Your word is a lamp for my feet and a light on my path.

Psalm 119:105 HCSB

More Great Ideas

Nobody ever outgrows Scripture; the book widens and deepens with our years.

C. H. Spurgeon

Faith is the virtue that enables us to believe and obey the Word of God, for faith comes from hearing and hearing from the Word of God.

Franklin Graham

Meditating upon His Word will inevitably bring peace of mind, strength of purpose, and power for living.

Bill Bright

Words fail to express my love for this holy Book, my gratitude for its author, for His love and goodness. How shall I thank him for it?

Lottie Moon

Weave the unveiling fabric of God's word through your heart and mind. It will hold strong, even if the rest of life unravels.

Gigi Graham Tchividjian

The great need of the hour
among persons spiritually
hungry is twofold:
First, to know the Scriptures,
apart from which no saving
truth will be vouchsafed
by our Lord; the second,
to be enlightened by the Spirit,
apart from whom
the Scriptures will not
be understood.

—

A. W. Tozer

Today's Timely Tip

Charles Swindoll writes, "There are four words I wish we would never forget, and they are, 'God keeps his word.'" And remember: When it comes to studying God's Word, school is always in session.

Today's Prayer

Heavenly Father, Your Holy Word is a light unto the world; let me study it, trust it, and share it with all who cross my path. In all that I do, help me be a worthy witness for You as I share the Good News of Your perfect Son and Your perfect Word. Amen

TODAY IS THE DAY!

This is the day the LORD has made;
we will rejoice and be glad in it.

—

Psalm 118:24 NKJV

The familiar words of Psalm 118:24 remind us that every day is a gift from God. Yet on some days, we don't feel much like celebrating. When the obligations of everyday living seem to overwhelm us, we may find ourselves frustrated by the demands of the present and worried by the uncertainty of the future.

When will you start celebrating life? Today or tomorrow? When will you thank God for His gifts—now or later? When will you accept the peace that can and should be yours? In the present moment or in the distant future? The answer, of course, is straightforward: the best moment to accept God's gifts is the present one.

There's an old saying—trite but true—"Today is the first day of the rest of your life." Whatever the days ahead may hold, keep God as your partner and Christ as your Savior. And every day, give thanks to the One who created you and saved you. God's love for you is infinite. Accept it joyously and be thankful.

Wisdom from God's Holy Word

Rejoice in the Lord always. I will say it again: Rejoice!

Philippians 4:4 HCSB

David and the whole house of Israel were celebrating before the Lord.

2 Samuel 6:5 HCSB

Their sorrow was turned into rejoicing and their mourning into a holiday. They were to be days of feasting, rejoicing, and of sending gifts to one another and the poor.

Esther 9:22 HCSB

At the dedication of the wall of Jerusalem, they sent for the Levites wherever they lived and brought them to Jerusalem to celebrate the joyous dedication with thanksgiving and singing accompanied by cymbals, harps, and lyres.

Nehemiah 12:27 HCSB

So teach us to number our days, that we may gain a heart of wisdom.

Psalm 90:12 NKJV

More Great Ideas

If you can forgive the person you were, accept the person you are, and believe in the person you will become, you are headed for joy. So celebrate your life.

Barbara Johnson

When the dream of our heart is one that God has planted there, a strange happiness flows into us. At that moment, all of the spiritual resources of the universe are released to help us. Our praying is then at one with the will of God and becomes a channel for the Creator's purposes for us and our world.

Catherine Marshall

Yesterday is the tomb of time, and tomorrow is the womb of time. Only now is yours.

R. G. Lee

Christ is the secret, the source, the substance, the center, and the circumference of all true and lasting gladness.

Mrs. Charles E. Cowman

Consider every day
as a new beginning,
the first day of your life,
and always act with
the same fervor.

—

St. Anthony of Padua

Today's Timely Tip

Today is a wonderful, one-of-a-kind gift from God. Treat it that way.

Today's Prayer

Lord, You have given me another day of life; let me celebrate this day, and let me use it according to Your plan. I praise You, Father, for my life and for the friends and family members who make it rich. Enable me to live each moment to the fullest as I give thanks for Your creation, for Your love, and for Your Son. Amen

THE RIGHT KIND OF ATTITUDE

*Your attitude should be the same as that of
Christ Jesus: Who, being in very nature God,
did not consider equality with God something to
be grasped, but made himself nothing, taking the
very nature of a servant, being made in human
likeness. And being found in appearance
as a man, he humbled himself and became
obedient to death—even death on a cross!*

—

Philippians 2:5-8 NIV

The Christian life is a cause for celebration, but sometimes we don't feel much like celebrating. In fact, when the weight of the world seems to bear down upon our shoulders, celebration may be the last thing on our minds . . . but it shouldn't be. As God's children, we are all blessed beyond measure on good days and bad. This day is a non-renewable resource—once it's gone, it's gone forever. We should give thanks for this day while using it for the glory of God.

What will your attitude be today? Will you be fearful, angry, bored, or worried? Will you be cynical, bitter, or pessimistic? If so, God wants to have a little talk with you.

God created you in His own image, and He wants you to experience joy and abundance. But, God will not force His joy upon you; you must claim it for yourself. So today, and every day hereafter, celebrate the life that God has given you. Think optimistically about yourself and your future. Give thanks to the One who has given you everything, and trust in your heart that He wants to give you so much more.

Wisdom from God's Holy Word

For the word of God is living and effective and sharper than any two-edged sword, penetrating as far as to divide soul, spirit, joints, and marrow; it is a judge of the ideas and thoughts of the heart.

Hebrews 4:12 HCSB

Make me to hear joy and gladness.

Psalm 51:8 KJV

Set your minds on what is above, not on what is on the earth.

Colossians 3:2 HCSB

A cheerful heart has a continual feast.

Proverbs 15:15 HCSB

More Great Ideas

A positive attitude will have positive results because attitudes are contagious.

Zig Ziglar

The people whom I have seen succeed best in life have always been cheerful and hopeful people who went about their business with a smile on their faces.

Charles Kingsley

If you can't tell whether your glass is half-empty of half-full, you don't need another glass; what you need is better eyesight . . . and a more thankful heart.

Marie T. Freeman

Life is 10% what happens to you and 90% how you respond to it.

Charles Swindoll

Life goes on. Keep on smiling and the whole world smiles with you.

Dennis Swanberg

The Reference Point for
the Christian is the Bible.
All values, judgments,
and attitudes must be gauged
in relationship to this
Reference Point.

—

Ruth Bell Graham

Today's Timely Tip

Attitudes are contagious, so it's important to associate with people who are upbeat, optimistic, and encouraging.

Today's Prayer

Dear Lord, I pray for an attitude that pleases You. In every circumstance, I will strive to celebrate the life You have given me . . . and I will praise You for Your priceless gifts. Amen

THE POWER OF ENCOURAGEMENT

*Anxiety in a man's heart weighs it down,
but a good word cheers it up.*

—

Proverbs 12:25 HCSB

Part of the art of friendship is learning the skill of encouraging others. And make no mistake: Encouragement is a skill that is learned over time and improved with constant use. As Christians, we are called upon to encourage one another, but sometimes we're not sure exactly what to say or do. How, we ask, can we be most encouraging? The answer is found, in part, by reminding ourselves what genuine encouragement is and what it is not.

The dictionary defines encouragement as, "the act of inspiring courage and confidence." As Christians, we must first seek to inspire others' confidence in God and in His Son Jesus Christ. We are comforted by the knowledge that God's gifts are too numerous to count and that His love extends to all generations—including our own. While our greatest encouragement comes from the assurance of God's power and His promises, we can also find encouragement when we are reminded of our own abilities and strengths. Genuine encouragement is not idle flattery; it is simply a firm reminder of talents that God has given each of us and of our need to use those talents wisely.

Genuine encouragement should never be confused with pity. God intends for His children to lead lives of abundance, joy, celebration, and praise—not lives of self-pity or regret. So we must guard ourselves against hosting or joining the "pity parties" that so often accompany difficult times. Instead, we must encourage each other to have faith—first in God and His only begotten Son—and then in our own abilities to use the talents God has given us for the furtherance of His kingdom and for the betterment of our own lives.

Wisdom from God's Holy Word

Carry one another's burdens; in this way you will fulfill the law of Christ.

Galatians 6:2 HCSB

I want their hearts to be encouraged and joined together in love, so that they may have all the riches of assured understanding, and have the knowledge of God's mystery—Christ.

Colossians 2:2 HCSB

More Great Ideas

The glory of friendship is not the outstretched hand, or the kindly smile, or the joy of companionship. It is the spiritual inspiration that comes to one when he discovers that someone else believes in him and is willing to trust him with his friendship.

Corrie ten Boom

God grant that we may not hinder those who are battling their way slowly into the light.

Oswald Chambers

We have the Lord, but He Himself has recognized that we need the touch of a human hand. He Himself came down and lived among us as a man. We cannot see Him now, but blessed be the tie that binds human hearts in Christian love.

Vance Havner

You can't light another's path without casting light on your own.

John Maxwell

Do you wonder where
you can go for encouragement
and motivation?
Run to Jesus.

—

Max Lucado

Today's Timely Tip

You should seek out encouraging friends who can lift you up, and you should strive to be an encouraging friend to others.

Today's Prayer

Dear Lord, let me celebrate the accomplishments of others. Make me a source of genuine, lasting encouragement to my family and friends. And let my words and deeds be worthy of Your Son, the One who gives me strength and salvation, this day and for all eternity. Amen

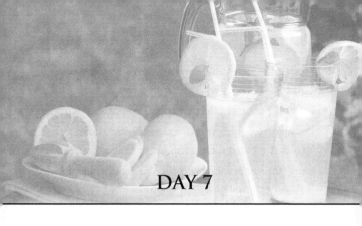

THE POWER OF PATIENCE

*Rejoice in hope; be patient in affliction;
be persistent in prayer.*

—

Romans 12:12 HCSB

We human beings are, by our very nature, impatient. We are impatient with others, impatient with ourselves, and impatient with our Creator. We want things to happen according to our own timetables, but our Heavenly Father may have other plans. That's why we must learn the art of patience.

Psalm 37:7 commands us to "rest in the Lord, and wait patiently for Him" (NKJV). But, for most of us, waiting patiently for Him is difficult. Why? Because we are fallible people who seek solutions to our problems today, if not sooner. Still, God instructs us to wait patiently for His plans to unfold, and that's exactly what we should do.

So the next time you find yourself drumming your fingers as you wait for a quick resolution to the challenges of everyday living, take a deep breath and ask God for patience. Be still before your Heavenly Father and trust His timetable: it's the peaceful way to live.

Wisdom from God's Holy Word

Love is patient; love is kind.

1 Corinthians 13:4 HCSB

A patient spirit is better than a proud spirit.

Ecclesiastes 7:8 HCSB

Therefore the Lord is waiting to show you mercy, and is rising up to show you compassion, for the Lord is a just God. Happy are all who wait patiently for Him.

Isaiah 30:18 HCSB

Be gentle to everyone, able to teach, and patient.

2 Timothy 2:23 HCSB

My brethren, count it all joy when you fall into various trials, knowing that the testing of your faith produces patience. But let patience have its perfect work, that you may be perfect and complete, lacking nothing.

James 1:2-4 NKJV

More Great Ideas

We must learn to wait. There is grace supplied to the one who waits.

Mrs. Charles E. Cowman

How do you wait upon the Lord? First you must learn to sit at His feet and take time to listen to His words.

Kay Arthur

Waiting is the hardest kind of work, but God knows best, and we may joyfully leave all in His hands.

Lottie Moon

Let me encourage you to continue to wait with faith. God may not perform a miracle, but He is trustworthy to touch you and make you whole where there used to be a hole.

Lisa Whelchel

Waiting is an essential part of spiritual discipline. It can be the ultimate test of faith.

Anne Graham Lotz

Let God use times of waiting to
mold and shape your character.
Let God use those times
to purify your life and
make you into a clean vessel
for His service.

—

Henry Blackaby and Claude King

Today's Timely Tip

With patience and faith, you can endure almost any hardship and overcome almost any setback. So be patient with yourself, with your situation, and with your Creator.

Today's Prayer

Lord, give me patience. When I am hurried, give me peace. When I am frustrated, give me perspective. When I am angry, let me turn my heart to You. Today, let me become a more patient friend, Dear Lord, as I trust in You and in Your master plan for my life. Amen

DAY 8

OPTIMISM NOW

Finally brothers, whatever is true, whatever is honorable, whatever is just, whatever is pure, whatever is lovely, whatever is commendable— if there is any moral excellence and if there is any praise—dwell on these things.

—

Philippians 4:8 HCSB

Pessimism and Christianity don't mix. Why? Because Christians have every reason to be optimistic about life here on earth and life eternal. Mrs. Charles E. Cowman advised, "Never yield to gloomy anticipation. Place your hope and confidence in God. He has no record of failure."

Sometimes, despite our trust in God, we may fall into the spiritual traps of worry, frustration, anxiety, or sheer exhaustion, and our hearts become heavy. What's needed is plenty of rest, a large dose of perspective, and God's healing touch.

Today, make this promise to yourself and keep it: vow to be a hope-filled Christian. Think optimistically about your life, your profession, and your future. Trust your hopes, not your fears. Take time to celebrate God's glorious creation. And then, when you've filled your heart with hope and gladness, share your optimism with others. They'll be better for it, and so will you. But not necessarily in that order.

Wisdom from God's Holy Word

Make me hear joy and gladness.

Psalm 51:8 NKJV

My cup runs over. Surely goodness and mercy shall follow me all the days of my life; and I will dwell in the house of the Lord Forever.

Psalm 23:5-6 NKJV

But if we hope for what we do not see, we eagerly wait for it with patience.

Romans 8:25 HCSB

For God has not given us a spirit of fearfulness, but one of power, love, and sound judgment.

2 Timothy 1:7 HCSB

Be strong and courageous, all you who put your hope in the LORD.

Psalm 31:24 HCSB

More Great Ideas

The Christian lifestyle is not one of legalistic do's and don'ts, but one that is positive, attractive, and joyful.

Vonette Bright

It never hurts your eyesight to look on the bright side of things.

Barbara Johnson

Make the least of all that goes and the most of all that comes. Don't regret what is past. Cherish what you have. Look forward to all that is to come. And most important of all, rely moment by moment on Jesus Christ.

Gigi Graham Tchividjian

We may run, walk, stumble, drive, or fly, but let us never lose sight of the reason for the journey, or miss a chance to see a rainbow on the way.

Gloria Gaither

Go forward confidently,
energetically attacking
problems, expecting
favorable outcomes.

—

Norman Vincent Peale

Today's Timely Tip

Be positive: If your thoughts tend toward the negative end of the spectrum, redirect them. How? You can start by counting your blessings and by thanking your Father in heaven. And while you're at it, train yourself to begin thinking thoughts that are more rational, more accepting, and more upbeat.

Today's Prayer

Dear Lord, I will look for the best in other people, I will expect the best from You, and I will try my best to do my best—today and every day. Amen

THE IMPORTANCE OF CHARACTER

As in water face reflects face,
so a man's heart reveals the man.

—

Proverbs 27:19 NKJV

Honesty is the best policy, but it is not always the easiest policy. Sometimes, the truth hurts, and sometimes, it's tough to be a person of integrity . . . tough, but essential.

Billy Graham observed, "Integrity is the glue that holds our way of life together. We must constantly strive to keep our integrity intact. When wealth is lost, nothing is lost; when health is lost, something is lost; when character is lost, all is lost." Loyal friends agree.

Integrity is built slowly over a lifetime. It is the sum of every right decision and every honest word. It is forged on the anvil of honorable work and polished by the twin virtues of honesty and fairness. Integrity is a precious thing—difficult to build but easy to tear down. As believers in Christ, we must seek to live each day with discipline, honesty, and faith. When we do, integrity becomes a habit. And God smiles.

Wisdom from God's Holy Word

As the water reflects the face, so the heart reflects the person.

Proverbs 27:19 HCSB

Do not be deceived: "Evil company corrupts good habits."

1 Corinthians 15:33 NKJV

We also rejoice in our afflictions, because we know that affliction produces endurance, endurance produces proven character, and proven character produces hope.

Romans 5:3-4 HCSB

Now don't be afraid, my daughter. I will do for you whatever you say, since all the people in my town know that you are a woman of noble character.

Ruth 3:11 HCSB

A good name is to be chosen rather than great riches, loving favor rather than silver and gold.

Proverbs 22:1 NKJV

More Great Ideas

The single most important element in any human relationship is honesty—with oneself, with God, and with others.

Catherine Marshall

There is no way to grow a saint overnight. Character, like the oak tree, does not spring up like a mushroom.

Vance Havner

Character is both developed and revealed by tests, and all of life is a test.

Rick Warren

Character is made in the small moments of our lives.

Phillips Brooks

Much guilt arises in the life of the believer from practicing the chameleon life of environmental adaptation.

Beth Moore

There's nothing like
the power of integrity.
It is a characteristic so radiant,
so steady, so consistent,
so beautiful, that it makes
a permanent picture
in our minds.

—

Franklin Graham

Today's Timely Tip

Character matters. Your ability to witness for Christ depends more upon your actions than your words.

_____

Today's Prayer

Dear Lord, make me a person whose conduct is honorable. Make me a friend whose words are true. Give me the wisdom to know right from wrong, and give me the courage—and the skill—to do what needs to be done in the service of Your Son. Amen

FINDING PEACE

*The peace of God, which surpasses
all understanding, will guard your hearts
and minds through Christ Jesus.*

—

Philippians 4:7 NKJV

Our world is in a state of constant change and so are we. God is not. At times, everything around us seems to be changing: our children are growing up, we are growing older, loved ones pass on. Sometimes, the world seems to be trembling beneath our feet. But we can be comforted in the knowledge that our Heavenly Father is the rock that cannot be shaken.

Are you at peace with the direction of your life? If you're a Christian, you should be. Perhaps you seek a new direction or a sense of renewed purpose, but those feelings should never rob you of the genuine peace that can and should be yours through a personal relationship with Jesus. The demands of everyday living should never obscure the fact that Christ died so that you might have life abundant and eternal.

Have you found the lasting peace that can be yours through Jesus, or are you still rushing after the illusion of "peace and happiness" that our world promises? The world's "peace" is fleeting; Christ's peace is forever.

Christ is standing at the door, waiting patiently for you to invite Him to reign in your heart. His eternal peace is offered freely. Claim it today.

Wisdom from God's Holy Word

Abundant peace belongs to those who love Your instruction; nothing makes them stumble.

Psalm 119:165 HCSB

If possible, on your part, live at peace with everyone.

Romans 12:18 HCSB

Blessed are the peacemakers, for they shall be called sons of God.

Matthew 5:9 NKJV

And suddenly there was with the angel a multitude of the heavenly host praising God and saying: "Glory to God in the highest, and on earth peace, goodwill toward men!"

Luke 2:13-14 NKJV

More Great Ideas

That peace, which has been described and which believers enjoy, is a participation of the peace which their glorious Lord and Master himself enjoys.

Jonathan Edwards

Peace is the deepest thing a human personality can know; it is almighty.

Oswald Chambers

We're prone to want God to change our circumstances, but He wants to change our character. We think that peace comes from the outside in, but it comes from the inside out.

Warren Wiersbe

Thou hast formed us for Thyself, and our hearts are restless till they find rest in Thee.

St. Augustine

What peace can they have who are not at peace with God?

Matthew Henry

First keep the peace
within yourself,
then you can also
bring peace to others.

—

Thomas à Kempis

Today's Timely Tip

Do you want to discover God's peace? Then do your best to live in the center of God's will.

_____

Today's Prayer

Dear Lord, You give me peace. I thank You, Father, for Your love, for Your peace, and for Your Son. Amen

THE RULE
THAT'S GOLDEN

*Therefore, whatever you want others
to do for you, do also the same for them—
this is the Law and the Prophets.*

—

Matthew 7:12 HCSB

The words of Matthew 7:12 remind us that, as believers in Christ, we are commanded to treat others as we wish to be treated. This commandment is, indeed, the Golden Rule for Christians of every generation.

Kindness is a choice. Sometimes, when we feel happy or prosperous, we find it easy to be kind. Other times, when we are discouraged or tired, we can scarcely summon the energy to utter a single kind word. But, God's commandment is clear: we must observe the Golden Rule "in everything." God intends that we make the conscious choice to treat others with kindness and respect, no matter our circumstances, no matter our emotions. Kindness, therefore, is a choice that we, as Christians must make many times each day.

When we weave the thread of kindness into the very fabric of our lives, we give a priceless gift to others, and we give glory to the One who gave His life for us. As believers, we must do no less.

Wisdom from God's Holy Word

Just as you want others to do for you, do the same for them.

Luke 6:31 HCSB

See that no one renders evil for evil to anyone, but always pursue what is good both for yourselves and for all.

1 Thessalonians 5:15 NKJV

If you really carry out the royal law prescribed in Scripture, You shall love your neighbor as yourself, you are doing well.

James 2:8 HCSB

And let us not grow weary while doing good, for in due season we shall reap if we do not lose heart.

Galatians 6:9 NKJV

For we are His workmanship, created in Christ Jesus for good works, which God prepared beforehand that we should walk in them.

Ephesians 2:10 NKJV

More Great Ideas

Before you can dry another's tears, you too must weep.

Barbara Johnson

Do all the good you can. By all the means you can. In all the ways you can. In all the places you can. At all the times you can. To all the people you can. As long as ever you can.

John Wesley

The Golden Rule starts at home, but it should never stop there.

Marie T. Freeman

Faith never asks whether good works are to be done, but has done them before there is time to ask the question, and it is always doing them.

Martin Luther

There is but one good; that is God. Everything else is good when it looks to Him and bad when it turns from Him.

C. S. Lewis

It is the duty of
every Christian to be
Christ to his neighbor.

—

Martin Luther

Today's Timely Tip

Remember this: when you treat others with respect, you won't just feel better about them, you'll feel better about yourself, too.

Today's Prayer

Dear Lord, because I expect kindness from others, let me be kind. Because I wish to be loved, let me be loving. Because I need forgiveness, let me be merciful. In all things, Lord, let me live by the Golden Rule that is the commandment of Your Son Jesus. Amen

DAY 12

CELEBRATING LIFE

This is the day the LORD has made;
we will rejoice and be glad in it.

—

Psalm 118:24 NKJV

A re you living a life of agitation, consternation, or celebration? If you're a believer, it should most certainly be the latter. With Christ as your Savior, every day should be a time of celebration.

Oswald Chambers correctly observed, "Joy is the great note all throughout the Bible." C. S. Lewis echoed that thought when he wrote, "Joy is the serious business of heaven." But, even the most dedicated Christians can, on occasion, forget to celebrate each day for what it is: a priceless gift from God.

Today, celebrate the life that God has given you. Today, put a smile on your face, kind words on your lips, and a song in your heart. Be generous with your praise and free with your encouragement. And then, when you have celebrated life to the fullest, invite your friends to do likewise. After all, this is God's day, and He has given us clear instructions for its use. We are commanded to rejoice and be glad. So, with no further ado, let the celebration begin . . .

Wisdom from God's Holy Word

David and the whole house of Israel were celebrating before the Lord.

2 Samuel 6:5 HCSB

Rejoice in the Lord always. I will say it again: Rejoice!

Philippians 4:4 HCSB

Their sorrow was turned into rejoicing and their mourning into a holiday. They were to be days of feasting, rejoicing, and of sending gifts to one another and the poor.

Esther 9:22 HCSB

At the dedication of the wall of Jerusalem, they sent for the Levites wherever they lived and brought them to Jerusalem to celebrate the joyous dedication with thanksgiving and singing accompanied by cymbals, harps, and lyres.

Nehemiah 12:27 HCSB

If they serve Him obediently, they will end their days in prosperity and their years in happiness.

Job 36:11 HCSB

More Great Ideas

We act as though comfort and luxury were the chief requirements of life, when all we need to make us really happy is something to be enthusiastic about.

Charles Kingsley

Our sense of joy, satisfaction, and fulfillment in life increases, no matter what the circumstances, if we are in the center of God's will.

Billy Graham

A child of God should be a visible beatitude for joy and a living doxology for gratitude.

C. H. Spurgeon

When we get rid of inner conflicts and wrong attitudes toward life, we will almost automatically burst into joy.

E. Stanley Jones

A life of intimacy with God is characterized by joy.

Oswald Chambers

The true joy of a man's life is
in his relationship to God.

—

Oswald Chambers

Today's Timely Tip

Every day is a glorious opportunity to place yourself in the service of the One who is the Giver of all blessings. When you celebrate God's gifts—when you place God's promises firmly in your mind and your heart—you'll find yourself celebrating life. And that, by the way, is exactly what God wants you to do.

Today's Prayer

Dear Lord, You have given me so many blessings, and as a way of saying "Thank You," I will celebrate. I will be a joyful Christian, Lord, quick to smile and slow to frown. And, I will share my joy with my family, with my friends, and with my neighbors, this day and every day. Amen

DAY 13

PRACTICAL
CHRISTIANITY

But be doers of the word and not hearers only.

—

James 1:22 HCSB

If we are to be loyal Christian friends, we must do our best to ensure that our actions are accurate reflections of our beliefs. Our theology must be demonstrated, not only by our words but, more importantly, by our actions. In short, we should be practical believers, quick to act whenever we see an opportunity to serve God.

Are you the kind of practical Christian who is willing to dig in and do what needs to be done when it needs to be done? If so, congratulations: God acknowledges your service and blesses it. But if you find yourself more interested in the fine points of theology than in the needs of your neighbors, it's time to rearrange your priorities. God needs believers who are willing to roll up their sleeves and go to work for Him. Count yourself among that number. Theology is a good thing unless it interferes with God's work. And it's up to you to make certain that your theology doesn't.

Wisdom from God's Holy Word

Therefore, get your minds ready for action, being self-disciplined, and set your hope completely on the grace to be brought to you at the revelation of Jesus Christ.

1 Peter 1:13 HCSB

When you make a vow to God, don't delay fulfilling it, because He does not delight in fools. Fulfill what you vow.

Ecclesiastes 5:4 HCSB

For the hearers of the law are not righteous before God, but the doers of the law will be declared righteous.

Romans 2:13 HCSB

Who is wise and understanding among you? He should show his works by good conduct with wisdom's gentleness.

James 3:13 HCSB

More Great Ideas

The church needs people who are doers of the Word and not just hearers.

Warren Wiersbe

Do noble things, do not dream them all day long.

Charles Kingsley

Paul did one thing. Most of us dabble in forty things. Are you a doer or a dabbler?

Vance Havner

Our Lord is searching for people who will make a difference. Christians dare not dissolve into the background or blend into the neutral scenery of the world.

Charles Swindoll

Let us not be content to wait and see what will happen, but give us the determination to make the right things happen.

Peter Marshall

Nothing is more disastrous
than to study faith,
analyze faith, make noble
resolves of faith,
but never actually to make
the leap of faith.

—

Vance Havner

Today's Timely Tip

The difference between theological dogma and faith with works is the difference between stagnant religion and joyful Christianity.

Today's Prayer

Dear Lord, I have heard Your Word, and I have felt Your presence in my heart; let me act accordingly. Let my words and deeds serve as a testimony to the changes You have made in my life. Let me praise You, Father, by following in the footsteps of Your Son, and let others see Him through me. Amen

DAY 14

NEIGHBORS

Jesus said unto him, Thou shalt love the Lord thy God with all thy heart, and with all thy soul, and with all thy mind. This is the first and great commandment. And the second is like unto it, Thou shalt love thy neighbor as thyself. On these two commandments hang all the law and the prophets.

—

Matthew 22:37-40 KJV

Neighbors. We know that we are instructed to love them, and yet there's so little time . . . and we're so busy. No matter. As Christians, we are commanded by our Lord and Savior Jesus Christ to love our neighbors just as we love ourselves. We are not asked to love our neighbors, nor are we encouraged to do so. We are commanded to love them. Period.

This very day, you will encounter someone who needs a word of encouragement, or a pat on the back, or a helping hand, or a heartfelt prayer. And, if you don't reach out to that person, who will? If you don't take the time to understand the needs of your neighbors, who will? If you don't love your brothers and sisters, who will? So, today, look for a neighbor in need . . . and then do something to help. Father's orders.

Wisdom from God's Holy Word

If I speak the languages of men and of angels, but do not have love, I am a sounding gong or a clanging cymbal.

1 Corinthians 13:1 HCSB

Now these three remain: faith, hope, and love. But the greatest of these is love.

1 Corinthians 13:13 HCSB

Dear friends, if God loved us in this way, we also must love one another. No one has ever seen God. If we love one another, God remains in us and His love is perfected in us.

1 John 4:11-12 HCSB

And we have this command from Him: the one who loves God must also love his brother.

1 John 4:21 HCSB

More Great Ideas

A person who really cares about his or her neighbor, a person who genuinely loves others, is a person who bears witness to the truth.

Anne Graham Lotz

That's a good part of the good old days—to be genuinely interested in your neighbor, and if you hear a distress signal, go see about him and his problem.

Jerry Clower

Wise Christians will be generous with their neighbors and live peaceably with them.

Warren Wiersbe

If my heart is right with God, every human being is my neighbor.

Oswald Chambers

Be so preoccupied with good will that you haven't room for ill will.

E. Stanley Jones

When we do little acts of
kindness that make life more
bearable for someone else,
we are walking in love as
the Bible commands us.

—

Barbara Johnson

Today's Timely Tip

To be a good neighbor, follow the Golden Rule. So treat your neighbors like you want to be treated. No exceptions.

Today's Prayer

Dear Lord, the Golden Rule is a perfect standard to use with my friends and neighbors. Help me to treat others as I wish to be treated. Let me be kind, fair, respectful, and generous. In all my dealings, let me be guided by the example of Christ so that I might glorify Your Son through my words, my deeds, my love for others . . . and my love for Him. Amen

TOO QUICK TO JUDGE?

Do not judge, and you will not be judged.
Do not condemn, and you will not be
condemned. Forgive, and you will be forgiven.

—

Luke 6:37 HCSB

Even the most loyal Christian friends may be quick to judge and slow to forgive. We human beings, imperfect as we are, seem all too quick to judge the actions and motivations of others. The temptation to judge is both powerful and subtle, but as Christians, we are commanded to refrain from such behavior. The warning of Matthew 7:1 is clear: "Judge not, that ye be not judged." But, as fallible, imperfect beings living in a stressful world, we are sorely tempted to do otherwise.

As Jesus came upon a young woman who had been condemned by the Pharisees, He spoke not only to the crowd that was gathered there, but also to all generations when He warned, "He that is without sin among you, let him first cast a stone at her" (John 8:7 KJV). Christ's message is clear, and it applies not only to the Pharisees of ancient times, but also to us.

We have all fallen short of God's commandments, and none of us, therefore, are qualified to "cast the first stone." Thankfully, God has forgiven us. We, too, must forgive others. When we do, we not only obey the commandments, we also free ourselves from the chains of bitterness and regret.

Wisdom from God's Holy Word

Speak and act as those who will be judged by the law of freedom. For judgment is without mercy to the one who hasn't shown mercy. Mercy triumphs over judgment.

James 2:12-13 HCSB

How can you say to your brother, "Brother, let me take out the speck that is in your eye," when you yourself don't see the log in your eye? Hypocrite! First take the log out of your eye, and then you will see clearly to take out the speck in your brother's eye.

Luke 6:42 HCSB

Therefore judge nothing before the time, until the Lord comes, who will both bring to light the hidden things of darkness and reveal the counsels of the hearts. Then each one's praise will come from God.

1 Corinthians 4:5 NKJV

More Great Ideas

I firmly believe a great many prayers are not answered because we are not willing to forgive someone.

D. L. Moody

God forgets the past. Imitate him.

Max Lucado

Christians think they are prosecuting attorneys or judges, when, in reality, God has called all of us to be witnesses.

Warren Wiersbe

An individual Christian may see fit to give up all sorts of things for special reasons—marriage, or meat, or beer, or cinema; but the moment he starts saying these things are bad in themselves, or looking down his nose at other people who do use them, he has taken the wrong turn.

C. S. Lewis

Turn your attention upon
yourself and beware of judging
the deeds of other men,
for in judging others a man
labors vainly, often makes
mistakes, and easily sins;
whereas, in judging and
taking stock of himself
he does something that is
always profitable.

—

Thomas à Kempis

Today's Timely Tip

To the extent you judge others, so, too, will you be judged. So you must, to the best of your ability, refrain from judgmental thoughts and words.

Today's Prayer

Lord, it's so easy to judge other people, but it's also easy to misjudge them. Only You can judge a human heart, Lord, so let me love my friends and neighbors, and let me help them, but never let me judge them. Amen

THE IMPORTANCE OF LAUGHTER

There is an occasion for everything, and a time
for every activity under heaven . . .
a time to weep and a time to laugh;
a time to mourn and a time to dance.

—

Ecclesiastes 3:1, 4 HCSB

Laughter is medicine for the soul, but sometimes, amid the stresses of the day, we forget to take our medicine. Instead of viewing our world with a mixture of optimism and humor, we allow worries and distractions to rob us of the joy that God intends for our lives.

So the next time you find yourself dwelling upon the negatives of life, refocus your attention to positive things. The next time you find yourself falling prey to the blight of pessimism, stop yourself and turn your thoughts around. And, if you see your glass as "half empty," rest assured that your spiritual vision is impaired. With God, your glass is never half empty. With God as your protector and Christ as your Savior, your glass is filled to the brim and overflowing . . . forever.

Today, as you go about your daily activities, approach life with a smile on your lips and hope in your heart. And laugh every chance you get. After all, God created laughter for a reason . . . and Father indeed knows best. So laugh!

Wisdom from God's Holy Word

A joyful heart makes a face cheerful.

Proverbs 15:13 HCSB

Oh, clap your hands, all you peoples! Shout to God with the voice of triumph!

Psalm 47:1 NKJV

The Lord reigns; let the earth rejoice.

Psalm 97:1 NKJV

I have spoken these things to you so that My joy may be in you and your joy may be complete.

John 15:11 HCSB

Blessed are you who are hungry now, because you will be filled. Blessed are you who weep now, because you will laugh.

Luke 6:21 HCSB

More Great Ideas

It is pleasing to the dear God whenever you rejoice or laugh from the bottom of your heart.

Martin Luther

I think everybody ought to be a laughing Christian. I'm convinced that there's just one place where there's not any laughter, and that's hell.

Jerry Clower

Laughter is to life what shock absorbers are to automobiles. It won't take the potholes out of the road, but it sure makes the ride smoother.

Barbara Johnson

Christ can put a spring in your step and a thrill in your heart. Optimism and cheerfulness are products of knowing Christ.

Billy Graham

Humor ought to be consecrated and used for the cause of Christ.

C. H. Spurgeon

When you have good, healthy
relationships with your family
and friends you're more
prompted to laugh and not
to take yourself so seriously.

—

Dennis Swanberg

Today's Timely Tip

Get everybody laughing! If family life is the cake, then laughter is the icing. And everybody in your clan deserves a slice with lots of icing.

Today's Prayer

Dear Lord, laughter is Your gift. Today and every day, put a smile on my face, and let me share that smile with all who cross my path . . . and let me laugh. Amen

HEALTHY RELATIONSHIPS

*The one who walks with the wise will become
wise, but a companion of fools will suffer harm.*

—

Proverbs 13:20 HCSB

Emotional health is contagious, and so is emotional distress. If you're fortunate enough to be surrounded by family members and friends who celebrate life and praise God, consider yourself profoundly blessed. But, if you find yourself caught in an unhealthy relationship, it's time to look realistically at your situation and begin making changes.

Don't worry about changing other people: you can't do it. What you can do is to conduct yourself in a responsible fashion and insist that other people treat you with the dignity and consideration that you deserve.

In a perfect world filled with perfect people, our relationships, too, would be perfect. But none of us are perfect and neither are our relationships . . . and that's okay. As we work to make our imperfect relationships a little happier and healthier, we grow as individuals and as families. But, if we find ourselves in relationships that are debilitating or dangerous, then changes must be made, and soon.

God has grand plans for your life; He has promised you the joy and abundance that can be yours through Him. But to fully experience God's gifts, you need happy, emotionally healthy people to share them with. It's up to you to make sure that you do your part to build the kinds of relationships that will bring abundance to you, to your family, and to God's world.

Wisdom from God's Holy Word

A wise man will hear and increase learning, and a man of understanding will attain wise counsel.

Proverbs 1:5 NKJV

Acquire wisdom—how much better it is than gold! And acquire understanding—it is preferable to silver.

Proverbs 16:16 HCSB

Now finally, all of you should be like-minded and sympathetic, should love believers, and be compassionate and humble.

1 Peter 3:8 HCSB

More Great Ideas

Line by line, moment by moment, special times are etched into our memories in the permanent ink of everlasting love in our relationships.

Gloria Gaither

I don't buy the cliché that quality time is the most important thing. If you don't have enough quantity, you won't get quality.

Leighton Ford

When you extend hospitality to others, you're not trying to impress people, you're trying to reflect God to them.

Max Lucado

It doesn't take monumental feats to make the world a better place. It can be as simple as letting someone go ahead of you in a grocery line.

Barbara Johnson

Horizontal relationships—
relationships between
people—are crippled at
the outset unless the vertical
relationship—the relationship
between each person and
God—is in place.

—

Ed Young

Today's Timely Tip

Sometimes people can be difficult, and sometimes friends misbehave. But it doesn't pay to get angry—your job is to be as understanding as possible. And while you're at it, remember that God wants you to forgive other folks, just like He forgives you.

_____

Today's Prayer

Dear Lord, You have brought family members and friends into my life. Let me love them, let me help them, let me treasure them, and let me lead them to You. Amen

DAY 18

FORGIVENESS NOW

All bitterness, anger and wrath, insult and
slander must be removed from you, along with
all wickedness. And be kind and compassionate
to one another, forgiving one another,
just as God also forgave you in Christ.

—

Ephesians 4:31-32 HCSB

I f we wish to build lasting friendships, we must learn how to forgive. Why? Because even our most beloved friends are imperfect (as are we).

Finding the generosity to forgive others is seldom easy, but if we truly desire to obey God's Word, we must learn to forgive our friends and family members, just as we wish to be forgiven by them. Until we learn the art of forgiveness, we remain trapped in prisons of our own resentment and regret.

If, in your heart, you hold bitterness against even a single person, forgive. If there exists even one person, alive or dead, whom you have not forgiven, follow God's commandment and His will for your life: forgive. If you are embittered against yourself for some past mistake or shortcoming, forgive. Then, to the best of your abilities, forget. And move on. Bitterness and regret are not part of God's plan for your life. Forgiveness is.

Wisdom from God's Holy Word

A person's insight gives him patience, and his virtue is to overlook an offense.

Proverbs 19:11 HCSB

See to it that no one repays evil for evil to anyone, but always pursue what is good for one another and for all.

1 Thessalonians 5:15 HCSB

And forgive us our sins, for we ourselves also forgive everyone in debt to us.

Luke 11:4 HCSB

Be merciful, just as your Father also is merciful.

Luke 6:36 HCSB

When they persisted in questioning Him, He stood up and said to them, "The one without sin among you should be the first to throw a stone at her."

John 8:7 HCSB

More Great Ideas

By not forgiving, by not letting wrongs go, we aren't getting back at anyone. We are merely punishing ourselves by barricading our own hearts.

Jim Cymbala

To hold on to hate and resentments is to throw a monkey wrench into the machinery of life.

E. Stanley Jones

Give me such love for God and men as will blot out all hatred and bitterness.

Dietrich Bonhoeffer

Our forgiveness toward others should flow from a realization and appreciation of God's forgiveness toward us.

Franklin Graham

The love of God is revealed in that He laid down His life for His enemies.

Oswald Chambers

Forgiveness is
a stunning principle,
your ticket out of hate
and fear and chaos.

—

Barbara Johnson

Today's Timely Tip

If forgiveness were easy, everybody would be doing it. But of course forgiveness can, at times, be a very hard thing to do. So be quick to forgive other people—even when it's difficult—is the correct thing to do.

Today's Prayer

Heavenly Father, give me a forgiving heart. When I am bitter, Your Word reminds me that forgiveness is Your commandment. Let me be Your obedient servant, Lord, and let me be a friend who forgives others just as You have forgiven me. Amen

COUNTING YOUR BLESSINGS

You will show me the path of life;
in Your presence is fullness of joy;
at Your right hand are pleasures forevermore.

—

Psalm 16:11 NKJV

If you sat down and began counting your blessings, how long would it take? A very, very long time! Your blessings include life, freedom, family, friends, talents, and possessions, for starters. But, your greatest blessing—a gift that is yours for the asking—is God's gift of salvation through Christ Jesus.

Are you a thankful believer who takes time each day to take a partial inventory of the gifts God has given you? Hopefully you are that kind of Christian. After all, God's Word makes it clear: a wise heart is a thankful heart.

We honor God, in part, by the genuine gratitude we feel in our hearts for the blessings He has bestowed upon us. Yet even the most saintly among us must endure periods of fear, doubt, and regret. Why? Because we are imperfect human beings who are incapable of perfect gratitude. Still, even on life's darker days, we must seek to cleanse our hearts of negative emotions and fill them, instead, with praise, with love, with hope, and with thanksgiving.

When the demands of life leave us rushing from place to place with scarcely a moment to spare, we may fail to pause and thank our Creator for His gifts. But, whenever we neglect to give proper thanks to the Father, we suffer because of our misplaced priorities.

Today, begin making a list of your blessings. You most certainly will not be able to make a complete list, but take a few moments and jot down as many blessings as you can. Then, give thanks to the Giver of all good things: God. His love for you is eternal, as are His gifts. And it's never too soon—or too late—to offer Him thanks.

Wisdom from God's Holy Word

I will make them and the area around My hill a blessing: I will send down showers in their season—showers of blessing.

Ezekiel 34:26 HCSB

Blessed is a man who endures trials, because when he passes the test he will receive the crown of life that He has promised to those who love Him.

James 1:12 HCSB

More Great Ideas

God's love for His children is unconditional, no strings attached. But, God's blessings on our lives do come with a condition—obedience. If we are to receive the fullness of God's blessings, we must obey Him and keep His commandments.

Jim Gallery

With the goodness of God to desire our highest welfare and the wisdom of God to plan it, what do we lack? Surely we are the most favored of all creatures.

A. W. Tozer

The Christian life is motivated, not by a list of do's and don'ts, but by the gracious outpouring of God's love and blessing.

Anne Graham Lotz

Blessings can either humble us and draw us closer to God or allow us to become full of pride and self-sufficiency.

Jim Cymbala

God is more anxious
to bestow His blessings on us
than we are to receive them.

—

St. Augustine

Today's Timely Tip

God wants to bless you abundantly and eternally. When you trust God completely and obey Him faithfully, you will be blessed.

Today's Prayer

Lord, You have given me so much, and I am thankful. Today, I seek Your blessings for my life, and I know that every good thing You give me is to be shared with others. I am blessed that I might be a blessing to those around me, Father. Let me give thanks for Your gifts . . . and let me share them. Amen

BEING A FAITHFUL STEWARD

Let a man so consider us, as servants of Christ and stewards of the mysteries of God. Moreover it is required in stewards that one be found faithful.

—

1 Corinthians 4:1-2 NKJV

D o you seek to be a righteous follower of Christ? Do you earnestly seek God's will for your life? And do you trust God's promises? If so, then you will be a faithful steward of the gifts He has given you.

Oswald Chambers advised, "Never support an experience which does not have God as its source, and faith in God as its result." And so it is with our tithes. When we return to God that which is rightfully His, we experience the spiritual growth that always accompanies obedience to Him. But, when we attempt to shortchange our Creator, either materially or spiritually, we distance ourselves from God. The consequences of our disobedience are as predictable as they are tragic.

As Christians, we are called to walk with God and to obey His commandments. To do so is an act of holiness. God deserves our obedience. May we obey Him in all things, including our tithes.

Wisdom from God's Holy Word

Well done, good and faithful servant; you were faithful over a few things, I will make you ruler over many things. Enter into the joy of your lord.

Matthew 25:21 NKJV

Based on the gift they have received, everyone should use it to serve others, as good managers of the varied grace of God.

1 Peter 4:10 HCSB

Every tenth of the land's produce, grain from the soil or fruit from the trees, belongs to the Lord; it is holy to the Lord.

Leviticus 27:30 HCSB

For I am the Lord, I do not change. . . . Will a man rob God? Yet you have robbed Me! But you say, in what way have we robbed You? In tithes and offerings. You are cursed with a curse, for you have robbed Me, even this whole nation. Bring all the tithes into the storehouse, that there may be food in My house.

Malachi 3:6, 8-10 NKJV

More Great Ideas

We are never more like God than when we give.

Charles Swindoll

Christians have become victims of one of the most devious plots Satan ever created—the concept that money belongs to us and not to God.

Larry Burkett

A steward does not own, but instead manages, all that his master puts into his hands.

Warren Wiersbe

Selfishness is as far from Christianity as darkness is from light.

C. H. Spurgeon

If our charities do not at all pinch or hamper us, I should say they are too small. There ought to be things we should like to do and cannot do because our charitable expenditure excludes them.

C. S. Lewis

Christians cannot experience peace in the area of finances until they have surrendered total control of this area to God and accepted their position as stewards.

—

Larry Burkett

Today's Timely Tip

A good steward knows that . . . everything comes from God, and everything God has is available to those who are good stewards.

Today's Prayer

Dear Lord, make me a faithful steward of my possessions, my talents, my time, and my testimony. In every aspect of my life, Father, let me be Your humble, obedient servant. I trust, Father, that You will provide for me now and throughout eternity. And I will obey Your commandment that I give sacrificially to the needs of Your Church. Amen

SHARING

So let each one give as he purposes in his heart,
not grudgingly or of necessity;
for God loves a cheerful giver.

—

2 Corinthians 9:7 NKJV

We live in a fast-paced, competitive world where it is easy to say, "Me first." But, God instructs us to do otherwise. In God's kingdom, those who proclaim, "Me first," are last. God loves a cheerful, selfless giver.

Sometimes, amid the busyness and distractions of everyday living, we may fail to share our possessions, our talents, or our time. Yet, God commands that we treat others as we wish to be treated. God's Word makes it clear: we must be generous with others just as we seek generosity for ourselves.

As believers in Christ, we are blessed here on earth, and we are blessed eternally through God's grace. We can never fully repay God for His gifts, but we can share them with others. When we give sacrificially, our blessings are multiplied . . . and so is our joy.

Wisdom from God's Holy Word

In every way I've shown you that by laboring like this, it is necessary to help the weak and to keep in mind the words of the Lord Jesus, for He said, "It is more blessed to give than to receive."

Acts 20:35 HCSB

Dear friend, you are showing your faith by whatever you do for the brothers, and this you are doing for strangers.

3 John 1:5 HCSB

If a brother or sister is without clothes and lacks daily food, and one of you says to them, "Go in peace, keep warm, and eat well," but you don't give them what the body needs, what good is it?

James 2:15–16 HCSB

The one who has two shirts must share with someone who has none, and the one who has food must do the same.

Luke 3:11 HCSB

More Great Ideas

Nothing is really ours until we share it.

C. S. Lewis

God shows unbridled delight when He sees people acting in ways that honor Him: when He receives worship, when He sees faith demonstrated in the most trying of circumstances, and when He sees tender love shared among His people.

Bill Hybels

Our faith grows by expression. If we want to keep our faith, we must share it. We must act.

Billy Graham

The best times in life are made a thousand times better when shared with a dear friend.

Luci Swindoll

The measure of a life, after all, is not its duration but its donation.

Corrie ten Boom

The rich man is not
one who possesses much,
but one who gives much.

—

St. John Chrysostom

Today's Timely Tip

God has given you countless blessings . . . and He wants you to share them.

Today's Prayer

Lord, make me a generous and cheerful friend. Help me to give generously of my time and my possessions as I care for my family, for my friends, and for those in need. And, make me a humble giver, Lord, so that all the glory and the praise might be Yours. Amen

ENTHUSIASM FOR THE JOURNEY

Whatever you do, do it enthusiastically,
as something done for the Lord and not for men.

—

Colossians 3:23 HCSB

Can you truthfully say that you are an enthusiastic person? Are you passionate about your faith, your life, your family, your friends, and your future? Hopefully so. But if your zest for life has waned, it is now time to redirect your efforts and recharge your spiritual batteries. And that means refocusing your priorities by putting God first.

Each day is a glorious opportunity to serve God and to do His will. Are you enthused about life, or do you struggle through each day giving scarcely a thought to God's blessings? Are you constantly praising God for His gifts, and are you sharing His Good News with the world? And are you excited about the possibilities for service that God has placed before you, whether at home, at work, or at church? You should be.

Nothing is more important than your wholehearted commitment to your Creator and to His only begotten Son. Your faith must never be an afterthought; it must be your ultimate priority, your ultimate possession, and your ultimate passion. When you become passionate about your faith, you'll become passionate about your life, too.

Norman Vincent Peale advised, "Get absolutely enthralled with something. Throw yourself into it with abandon. Get out of yourself. Be somebody. Do something." His words apply to you. So don't settle for a lukewarm existence. Instead, make the choice to become genuinely involved in life. The world needs your enthusiasm . . . and so do you.

Wisdom from God's Holy Word

I have seen that there is nothing better than for a person to enjoy his activities, because that is his reward. For who can enable him to see what will happen after he dies?

Ecclesiastes 3:22 HCSB

He did it with all his heart. So he prospered.

2 Chronicles 31:21 NKJV

Render service with a good attitude, as to the Lord and not to men.

Ephesians 6:7 HCSB

More Great Ideas

Your light is the truth of the Gospel message itself as well as your witness as to Who Jesus is and what He has done for you. Don't hide it.

Anne Graham Lotz

Making up a string of excuses is usually harder than doing the work.

Marie T. Freeman

Living life with a consistent spiritual walk deeply influences those we love most.

Vonette Bright

God is the giver, and we are the receivers. And His richest gifts are bestowed not upon those who do the greatest things, but upon those who accept His abundance and His grace.

Hannah Whitall Smith

Enthusiasm, like the flu, is contagious—we get it from one another.

Barbara Johnson

If our hearts have been attuned to God through an abiding faith in Christ, the result will be joyous optimism and good cheer.

—

Billy Graham

Today's Timely Tip

Don't wait for enthusiam to find you . . . go looking for it. Look at your life and your relationships as exciting adventures. Don't wait for life to spice itself; spice things up yourself.

Today's Prayer

Dear Lord, I know that others are watching the way that I live my life. Help me to be an enthusiastic Christian with a faith that is contagious. Amen.

DAY 23

BE STILL MY SOUL

Be still, and know that I am God . . . .

—

Psalm 46:10 KJV

A re you so busy that you rush through the day with scarcely a single moment for quiet contemplation and prayer? If so, it's time to reorder your priorities.

We live in a noisy world, a world filled with distractions, frustrations, and complications. But if we allow the distractions of a clamorous world to separate us from God's peace, we do ourselves a profound disservice. If we are to maintain righteous minds and compassionate hearts, we must take time each day for prayer and for meditation. We must make ourselves still in the presence of our Creator. We must quiet our minds and our hearts so that we might sense God's will, God's love, and God's Son.

Has the busy pace of life robbed you of the peace that might otherwise be yours through Jesus Christ? Nothing is more important than the time you spend with your Savior. So be still and claim the inner peace that is your spiritual birthright: the peace of Jesus Christ. It is offered freely; it has been paid for in full; it is yours for the asking. So ask. And then share.

Wisdom from God's Holy Word

Be silent before Me.

Isaiah 41:1 HCSB

Be silent before the Lord and wait expectantly for Him.

Psalm 37:7 HCSB

Truly my soul silently waits for God; from Him comes my salvation.

Psalm 62:1 NKJV

My soul, wait silently for God alone, For my expectation is from Him.

Psalm 62:5 NKJV

But those who wait on the Lord shall renew their strength; they shall mount up with wings like eagles, they shall run and not be weary, they shall walk and not faint.

Isaiah 40:31 NKJV

More Great Ideas

When we are in the presence of God, removed from distractions, we are able to hear
him more clearly, and a secure environment
has been established for the young and broken
places in our hearts to surface.

John Eldredge

The world is full of noise. Might we not set
ourselves to learn silence, stillness, solitude?

Elisabeth Elliot

Because Jesus Christ is our Great High Priest,
not only can we approach God without a human "go-between," we can also hear and learn
from God in some sacred moments without
one.

Beth Moore

Let your loneliness be transformed into a holy
aloneness. Sit still before the Lord. Remember
Naomi's word to Ruth: "Sit still, my daughter,
until you see how the matter will fall."

Elisabeth Elliot

When frustrations develop
into problems that stress
you out, the best way to cope is
to stop, catch your breath,
and do something for yourself,
not out of selfishness,
but out of wisdom.

—

Barbara Johnson

Today's Timely Tip

Try this experiment: the next time you're driving alone in your automobile, do so without the radio, CDs, or cell phones. And then, have a quiet talk with God about His plans for your life. You may be surprised to discover that sometimes the most important answers are the ones you receive in silence.

Today's Prayer

Dear Lord, let me be still before You. When I am hurried or distracted, slow me down and redirect my thoughts. When I am confused, give me perspective. Keep me mindful, Father, that You are always with me. And let me sense Your presence today, tomorrow, and forever. Amen

BELIEVE IN YOURSELF!

For You have made him a little lower than the angels, and You have crowned him with glory and honor.

—

Psalm 8:5 NKJV

D o you believe that you deserve the best, and that you can achieve the best? Or have you convinced yourself that you're a second-tier talent who'll be lucky to finish far back in the pack? Before you answer that question, remember this: God sent His Son so that you might enjoy the abundant life that Jesus describes in the familiar words of John 10:10. But, God's gifts are not guaranteed—it's up to you to claim them.

Make a promise to yourself that when it comes to the important things in life, you won't settle for second best. And what, pray tell, are the "important things"? Your faith, your family, your health, and your relationships, for starters. In each of these areas, you deserve to be a rip-roaring, top-drawer success.

So if you want to achieve the best that life has to offer, convince yourself that you have the ability to earn the rewards you desire. Become sold on yourself—sold on your opportunities, sold on your potential, sold on your abilities. If you're sold on yourself, chances are the world will soon become sold too, and the results will be beautiful.

Wisdom from God's Holy Word

*How happy are those whose way is blameless,
who live according to the law of the Lord! Happy
are those who keep His decrees and seek Him with
all their heart.*

Psalm 119:1-2 HCSB

If God is for us, who is against us?

Romans 8:31 HCSB

*Finally, brethren, whatever things are true,
whatever things are noble, whatever things are
just, whatever things are pure, whatever things
are lovely, whatever things are of good report,
if there is any virtue and if there is anything
praiseworthy—meditate on these things.*

Philippians 4:8 NKJV

*For it was You who created my inward parts;
You knit me together in my mother's womb. I will
praise You, because I have been remarkably and
wonderfully made. Your works are wonderful,
and I know [this] very well.*

Psalm 139:13-14 HCSB

More Great Ideas

When it comes to our position before God, we're perfect. When he sees each of us, he sees one who has been made perfect through the One who is perfect—Jesus Christ.

Max Lucado

Being loved by Him whose opinion matters most gives us the security to risk loving, too— even loving ourselves.

Gloria Gaither

Give yourself a gift today: be present with yourself. God is. Enjoy your own personality. God does.

Barbara Johnson

The Creator has made us each one of a kind. There is nobody else exactly like us, and there never will be. Each of us is his special creation and is alive for a distinctive purpose.

Luci Swindoll

Do not wish to be anything
but what you are,
and try to be that perfectly.

—

St. Francis of Sales

Today's Timely Tip

Old-fashioned respect never goes out of style—respect for other people and respect for the person in the mirror.

Today's Prayer

Dear Lord, thank You for Your Son. Because Jesus loves me, I will feel good about myself, my family, and my future. Amen

DAY 25

GOD'S LOVE

*But God demonstrates His own love toward us,
in that while we were still sinners,
Christ died for us.*

—

Romans 5:8 NKJV

You know the profound love that you hold in your heart for your family and friends. As a child of God, you can only imagine the infinite love that your Heavenly Father has for you.

Today, what will you do in response to God's love? Will you live purposefully and joyfully? Will you celebrate God's creation while giving thanks for His blessings? And will you share God's love with family members, friends, and even strangers? Hopefully so. After all, God's message—and His love—are meant to be shared.

Your Heavenly Father—a God of infinite love and mercy—is waiting to embrace you with open arms. Accept His love, and share it, today . . . and forever.

Wisdom from God's Holy Word

May he be blessed by the Lord, who has not forsaken his kindness to the living or the dead.

Ruth 2:20 HCSB

For God loved the world in this way: He gave His only Son, so that everyone who believes in Him will not perish but have eternal life.

John 3:16 HCSB

Whoever is wise will observe these things, and they will understand the lovingkindness of the Lord.

Psalm 107:43 NKJV

But God, who is abundant in mercy, because of His great love that He had for us, made us alive with the Messiah even though we were dead in trespasses. By grace you are saved!

Ephesians 2:4-5 HCSB

We love Him because He first loved us.

1 John 4:19 NKJV

157

More Great Ideas

There is no pit so deep that God's love is not deeper still.

Corrie ten Boom

I love Him because He first loved me, and He still does love me, and He will love me forever and ever.

Bill Bright

The hope we have in Jesus is the anchor for the soul—something sure and steadfast, preventing drifting or giving way, lowered to the depth of God's love.

Franklin Graham

Sometimes Agape really hurts. It broke the heart of God to demonstrate His love to us through Christ, but its ultimate end was salvation.

Beth Moore

It was not the soldiers who killed him, nor the screams of the mob: It was his devotion to us.

Max Lucado

Even before God created
the heavens and the earth,
He knew you and me,
and He chose us!
You and I were born because
it was God's good pleasure.

—

Kay Arthur

Today's Timely Tip

Demonstrate the importance of your relationship with God by spending time with Him each day. And take time each day to share God's love with your family and friends.

Today's Prayer

Thank You, Lord, for Your love. Your love is boundless, infinite, and eternal. Today, let me pause and reflect upon Your love for me, and let me share that love with all those who cross my path. And, as an expression of my love for You, Father, let me share the saving message of Your Son with a world in desperate need of His peace. Amen

DAY 26

BE HOPEFUL

For I know the thoughts that I think toward you,
says the Lord, thoughts of peace and not of evil,
to give you a future and a hope. Then you will
call upon Me and go and pray to Me,
and I will listen to you.

—

Jeremiah 29:11-12 NKJV

Have you ever felt hope for the future slipping away? If so, you have temporarily lost sight of the hope that we, as believers, must place in the promises of our Heavenly Father. If you are feeling discouraged, worried, or worse, remember the words of Psalm 31: "Be of good courage, and He shall strengthen your heart."

Because we are saved by a risen Christ, we can have hope for the future, no matter how desperate our circumstances may seem. After all, God has promised that we are His throughout eternity. And, He has told us that we must place our hopes in Him.

Of course, we will face disappointments and failures, but these are only temporary defeats. Of course, this world can be a place of trials and tribulations, but we are secure. God has promised us peace, joy, and eternal life. And God keeps His promises today, tomorrow, and forever.

Wisdom from God's Holy Word

Now may the God of hope fill you with all joy and peace in believing, so that you may overflow with hope by the power of the Holy Spirit.

Romans 15:13 HCSB

But if we hope for what we do not see, we eagerly wait for it with patience.

Romans 8:25 HCSB

Rejoice in hope; be patient in affliction; be persistent in prayer.

Romans 12:12 HCSB

Lord, I turn my hope to You. My God, I trust in You. Do not let me be disgraced; do not let my enemies gloat over me.

Psalm 25:1-2 HCSB

Let us hold on to the confession of our hope without wavering, for He who promised is faithful.

Hebrews 10:23 HCSB

More Great Ideas

People are genuinely motivated by hope and a part of that hope is the assurance of future glory with God for those who are His people.

Warren Wiersbe

Our hope in Christ for the future is the mainstream of our joy.

C. H. Spurgeon

Oh, remember this: There is never a time when we may not hope in God. Whatever our necessities, however great our difficulties, and though to all appearance help is impossible, yet our business is to hope in God, and it will be found that it is not in vain.

George Mueller

The hope we have in Jesus is the anchor for the soul—something sure and steadfast, preventing drifting or giving way, lowered to the depth of God's love.

Franklin Graham

Hope looks for the good in
people, opens doors for people,
discovers what can be done
to help, lights a candle,
does not yield to cynicism.
Hope sets people free.

—

Barbara Johnson

Today's Timely Tip

If you're experiencing hard times, you'll be wise to start spending more time with God. And if you do your part, God will do His part. So never be afraid to hope—or to ask—for a miracle.

Today's Prayer

Dear Lord, make me a person of hope. If I become discouraged, let me turn to You. If I grow weary, let me seek strength in You. When I face adversity, let me seek Your will and trust Your Word. In every aspect of my life, I will trust You, Father, so that my heart will be filled with faith and hope, this day and forever. Amen

RELATIONSHIPS THAT ARE BUILT UPON TRUST

Lead a quiet and peaceable life
in all godliness and honesty.

—

1 Timothy 2:2 KJV

L asting relationships are built upon a firm foundation of honesty and trust. Temporary relationships are built upon the shifting sands of deception and insincerity. Which foundation will you choose?

It has been said on many occasions that honesty is the best policy. But for Christians, it is far more important to note that honesty is God's policy. And if we are to be servants worthy of our Savior, we must be honest and forthright in all our communications with others.

Sometimes, honesty is difficult; sometimes, honesty is painful; sometimes, honesty makes us feel uncomfortable. Despite these temporary feelings of discomfort, we must make honesty the hallmark of all our relationships; otherwise, we invite needless suffering into our own lives and into the lives of those we love.

Sometime soon, perhaps even today, you will be tempted to bend the truth or to break it. Resist that temptation. Truth is God's way . . . and it must be your way, too.

Wisdom from God's Holy Word

The just man walketh in his integrity: his children are blessed after him.

Proverbs 20:7 KJV

These are the things you must do: Speak truth to one another; render honest and peaceful judgments in your gates.

Zechariah 8:16 HCSB

Above all, put on love—the perfect bond of unity.

Colossians 3:14 HCSB

Behold, how good and how pleasant it is for brethren to dwell together in unity!

Psalm 133:1 NKJV

Do not be unequally yoked together with unbelievers. For what fellowship has righteousness with lawlessness? And what communion has light with darkness?

2 Corinthians 6:14 NKJV

More Great Ideas

God never called us to naïveté. He called us to integrity. The biblical concept of integrity emphasizes mature innocence not childlike ignorance.

Beth Moore

Integrity is a sign of maturity.

Charles Swindoll

Maintaining your integrity in a world of sham is no small accomplishment.

Wayne Oates

There's nothing like the power of integrity. It is a characteristic so radiant, so steady, so consistent, so beautiful, that it makes a permanent picture in our minds.

Franklin Graham

The commandment of absolute truthfulness is really only another name for the fullness of discipleship.

Dietrich Bonhoeffer

One thing that is important
for stable emotional health
is honesty—
with self and with others.

—

Joyce Meyer

Today's Timely Tip

Lasting relationships are built upon trust. If you want your relationships to last, you must be honest and trustworthy.

Today's Prayer

Dear Lord, You command Your children to walk in truth. Let me be honest with my family and friends, and let me be honest with myself. Honesty isn't just the best policy, Lord; it's Your policy, and I will obey You by making it my policy, too. Amen

BEYOND WORRY

*Don't worry about anything, but in everything,
through prayer and petition with thanksgiving,
let your requests be made known to God.*

—

Philippians 4:6 HCSB

Here's a riddle: What is it that is too unimportant to pray about yet too big for God to handle? The answer, of course, is: "nothing." Yet sometimes, when the challenges of the day seem overwhelming, we may spend more time worrying about our troubles than praying about them. And, we may spend more time fretting about our problems than solving them. A far better strategy is to pray as if everything depended entirely upon God and to work as if everything depended entirely upon us.

What we see as problems God sees as opportunities. And if we are to trust Him completely, we must acknowledge that even when our own vision is dreadfully impaired, His vision is perfect.

Today and every day, let us trust God by courageously confronting the things that we see as problems and He sees as possibilities. And while we're at it, let's remind our friends and family members that no problem is too big for God . . . not even our problems.

Wisdom from God's Holy Word

Your heart must not be troubled. Believe in God; believe also in Me.

John 14:1 HCSB

Come to Me, all you who labor and are heavy laden, and I will give you rest. Take My yoke upon you and learn from Me, for I am gentle and lowly in heart, and you will find rest for your souls. For My yoke is easy and My burden is light.

Matthew 11:28-30 NKJV

I will be with you when you pass through the waters . . . when you walk through the fire . . . the flame will not burn you. For I the Lord your God, the Holy One of Israel, and your Savior.

Isaiah 43:2-3 HCSB

Don't worry about your life, what you will eat or what you will drink; or about your body, what you will wear. Isn't life more than food and the body more than clothing?

Matthew 6:25 HCSB

More Great Ideas

God is bigger than your problems. Whatever worries press upon you today, put them in God's hands and leave them there.

Billy Graham

The beginning of anxiety is the end of faith, and the beginning of true faith is the end of anxiety.

George Mueller

Today is mine. Tomorrow is none of my business. If I peer anxiously into the fog of the future, I will strain my spiritual eyes so that I will not see clearly what is required of me now.

Elisabeth Elliott

We are not called to be burden-bearers, but cross-bearers and light-bearers. We must cast our burdens on the Lord.

Corrie ten Boom

I've read the last page
of the Bible.
It's all going to turn out
all right.

—

Billy Graham

Today's Timely Tip

An important part of becoming a more mature Christian is learning to worry less and to trust God more.

Today's Prayer

Forgive me, Lord, when I worry. Worry reflects a lack of trust in Your ability to meet my every need. Help me to work, Lord, and not to worry. And, keep me mindful, Father, that nothing, absolutely nothing, will happen this day that You and I cannot handle together. Amen

THE GREATEST
OF THESE . . .

Now these three remain: faith, hope, and love.
But the greatest of these is love.

—

1 Corinthians 13:13 HCSB

Make no mistake: you are loved. Your family loves you, your closest friends love you, and God loves you. How will you respond to their love? Jesus clearly defined what your response should be: "'Love the Lord your God with all your heart and with all your soul and with all your mind.' This is the first and greatest commandment. And the second is like it: 'Love your neighbor as yourself.' All the Law and the Prophets hang on these two commandments" (Matthew 22:37-40 NIV).

Today, as you meet the demands of everyday living, will you pause long enough to return God's love? And then will you share it? Prayerfully, you will. When you embrace God's love, you are forever changed. When you embrace God's love, you feel differently about yourself, your family, your friends, and your world. When you embrace God's love, you have enough love to keep and enough love to share: enough love for a day, enough love for a lifetime, enough love for all eternity.

Wisdom from God's Holy Word

I pray that you, being rooted and firmly established in love, may be able to comprehend with all the saints what is the breadth and width, height and depth, and to know the Messiah's love that surpasses knowledge, so you may be filled with all the fullness of God.

Ephesians 3:17-19 HCSB

If I speak the languages of men and of angels, but do not have love, I am a sounding gong or a clanging cymbal.

1 Corinthians 13:1 HCSB

Dear friends, if God loved us in this way, we also must love one another.

1 John 4:11 HCSB

We love because He first loved us.

1 John 4:19 HCSB

Above all, keep your love for one another at full strength, since love covers a multitude of sins.

1 Peter 4:8 HCSB

More Great Ideas

Love is not soft as water is; it is solid as a rock on which the waves of hatred beat in vain.

Corrie ten Boom

Love always means sacrifice.

Elisabeth Elliot

Line by line, moment by moment, special times are etched into our memories in the permanent ink of everlasting love in our relationships.

Gloria Gaither

Love is extravagant in the price it is willing to pay, the time it is willing to give, the hardships it is willing to endure, and the strength it is willing to spend. Love never thinks in terms of "how little," but always in terms of "how much." Love gives, love knows, and love lasts.

Joni Eareckson Tada

Love is not grabbing,
or self-centered, or selfish.
Real love is being able to
contribute to the happiness
of another person without
expecting to get
anything in return.

—

James Dobson

Today's Timely Tip

The key to successful Christian living lies in your submission to the Spirit of God. If you're a Christian, God has commanded you to love people . . . and it's a commandment that covers both saints and sinners.

Today's Prayer

Dear God, let me share Your love with the world. Help me to recognize the needs of others. Let me forgive those who have hurt me, just as You have forgiven me. And let the love of Your Son shine in me and through me today, tomorrow, and throughout all eternity. Amen

FOR GOD SO LOVED THE WORLD

For God so loved the world, that he gave his only begotten Son, that whosoever believeth in him should not perish, but have everlasting life.

—

John 3:16 KJV

God's grace is not earned . . . thank goodness! To earn God's love and His gift of eternal life would be far beyond the abilities of even the most righteous man or woman. Thankfully, grace is not an earthly reward for righteous behavior; it is a blessed spiritual gift which can be accepted by believers who dedicate themselves to God through Christ. When we accept Christ into our hearts, we are saved by His grace.

The familiar words of Ephesians 2:8 make God's promise perfectly clear: It is by grace we have been saved, through faith. We are saved not because of our good deeds but because of our faith in Christ.

God's grace is the ultimate gift, and we owe to Him the ultimate in thanksgiving. Let us praise the Creator for His priceless gift, and let us share the Good News with all who cross our paths. We return our Father's love by accepting His grace and by sharing His message and His love.

Have you thanked God today for blessings that are too numerous to count? Have you offered Him your heartfelt prayers and your wholehearted praise? If not, it's time to slow down and offer a prayer of thanksgiving to the One who has given you life on earth and life eternal.

If you are a thoughtful Christian, you will be a thankful Christian. No matter your circumstances, you owe God so much more than you can ever repay, and you owe Him your heartfelt thanks. So thank Him . . . and keep thanking Him, today, tomorrow and forever.

Wisdom from God's Holy Word

Therefore let us approach the throne of grace with boldness, so that we may receive mercy and find grace to help us at the proper time.

Hebrews 4:16 HCSB

Therefore, since we are receiving a kingdom that cannot be shaken, let us hold on to grace. By it, we may serve God acceptably, with reverence and awe.

Hebrews 12:28 HCSB

More Great Ideas

When I consider my existence beyond the grace, I am filled with confidence and gratitude because God has made an inviolable commitment to take me to heaven on the merits of Christ.

Bill Hybels

When you experience grace and are loved when you do not deserve it, you spend the rest of your life standing on tiptoes trying to reach His plan for your life out of gratitude.

Charles Stanley

While grace cannot grow more, we can grow more in it.

C. H. Spurgeon

Once grace has scrubbed the soul, anyone can take their place in the lineage of the Son of God.

Calvin Miller

He is the same yesterday,
today, and forever,
and His unchanging and
unfailing love sustains me
when nothing and
no one else can.

—

Bill Bright

Today's Timely Tip

God's grace is always available. Jim Cymbala writes, "No one is beyond his grace. No situation, anywhere on earth, is too hard for God." If you sincerely seek God's grace, He will give it freely. So ask, and you will receive.

Today's Prayer

Accepting Your grace can be hard, Lord. Somehow, I feel that I must earn Your love and Your acceptance. Yet, the Bible promises that You love me and save me by Your grace. It is a gift I can only accept and cannot earn. Thank You for Your priceless, everlasting gift. Amen

MORE FROM
GOD'S WORD
ABOUT . . .

Anger

A patient person [shows] great understanding, but a quick-tempered one promotes foolishness.

Proverbs 14:29 HCSB

But now you must also put away all the following: anger, wrath, malice, slander, and filthy language from your mouth.

Colossians 3:8 HCSB

All bitterness, anger and wrath, insult and slander must be removed from you, along with all wickedness. And be kind and compassionate to one another, forgiving one another, just as God also forgave you in Christ.

Ephesians 4:31-32 HCSB

Everyone must be quick to hear, slow to speak, and slow to anger, for man's anger does not accomplish God's righteousness.

James 1:19-20 HCSB

*Don't let your spirit rush
to be angry, for anger abides
in the heart of fools.*

—

Ecclesiastes 7:9 HCSB

Attitude

For the word of God is living and effective and sharper than any two-edged sword, penetrating as far as to divide soul, spirit, joints, and marrow; it is a judge of the ideas and thoughts of the heart.

Hebrews 4:12 HCSB

Make your own attitude that of Christ Jesus.

Philippians 2:5 HCSB

Set your minds on what is above, not on what is on the earth.

Colossians 3:2 HCSB

Finally brothers, whatever is true, whatever is honorable, whatever is just, whatever is pure, whatever is lovely, whatever is commendable—if there is any moral excellence and if there is any praise—dwell on these things.

Philippians 4:8 HCSB

Cheerfulness

A merry heart does good, like medicine.

Proverbs 17:22 NKJV

Is anyone cheerful? He should sing praises.

James 5:13 HCSB

A cheerful heart has a continual feast.

Proverbs 15:15 HCSB

Bright eyes cheer the heart; good news strengthens the bones.

Proverbs 15:30 HCSB

A joyful heart makes a face cheerful.

Proverbs 15:13 HCSB

Faith

If you do not stand firm in your faith, then you will not stand at all.

Isaiah 7:9 HCSB

Be alert, stand firm in the faith, be brave and strong.

1 Corinthians 16:13 HCSB

Now faith is the reality of what is hoped for, the proof of what is not seen.

Hebrews 11:1 HCSB

For we walk by faith, not by sight.

2 Corinthians 5:7 HCSB

Now without faith it is impossible to please God, for the one who draws near to Him must believe that He exists and rewards those who seek Him.

Hebrews 11:6 HCSB

Family

Choose for yourselves today the one you will worship . . . . As for me and my family, we will worship the Lord.

Joshua 24:15 HCSB

Now if anyone does not provide for his own relatives, and especially for his household, he has denied the faith and is worse than an unbeliever.

1 Timothy 5:8 HCSB

If a kingdom is divided against itself, that kingdom cannot stand. If a house is divided against itself, that house cannot stand.

Mark 3:24-25 HCSB

Love must be without hypocrisy. Detest evil; cling to what is good. Show family affection to one another with brotherly love. Outdo one another in showing honor.

Romans 12:9–10 HCSB

Loving God

He said to him, "You shall love the Lord your God with all your heart, with all your soul, and with all your mind. This is the greatest and most important commandment."

Matthew 22:37-38 HCSB

And we have this command from Him: the one who loves God must also love his brother.

1 John 4:21 HCSB

Love the Lord your God with all your heart, with all your soul, and with all your strength. These words that I am giving you today are to be in your heart. Repeat them to your children. Talk about them when you sit in your house and when you walk along the road, when you lie down and when you get up.

Deuteronomy 6:5-7 HCSB

For this is the love of God, that we keep His commandments. And His commandments are not burdensome.

1 John 5:3 NKJV

*We love Him
because He first loved us.*

—

1 John 4:19 NKJV

Materialism

And He told them, "Watch out and be on guard against all greed, because one's life is not in the abundance of his possessions."

Luke 12:15 HCSB

For what does it benefit a man to gain the whole world yet lose his life? What can a man give in exchange for his life?

Mark 8:36-37 HCSB

Don't collect for yourselves treasures on earth, where moth and rust destroy and where thieves break in and steal. But collect for yourselves treasures in heaven, where neither moth nor rust destroys, and where thieves don't break in and steal. For where your treasure is, there your heart will be also.

Matthew 6:19-21 HCSB

For the mind-set of the flesh is death, but the mind-set of the Spirit is life and peace.

Romans 8:6 HCSB

Anyone trusting
in his riches will fall,
but the righteous
will flourish like foliage.

—

Proverbs 11:28 HCSB

Temptation

No temptation has overtaken you except what is common to humanity. God is faithful and He will not allow you to be tempted beyond what you are able, but with the temptation He will also provide a way of escape, so that you are able to bear it.

1 Corinthians 10:13 HCSB

For we do not have a High Priest who cannot sympathize with our weaknesses, but was in all points tempted as we are, yet without sin. Let us therefore come boldly to the throne of grace, that we may obtain mercy and find grace to help in time of need.

Hebrews 4:15-16 NKJV

Be sober! Be on the alert! Your adversary the Devil is prowling around like a roaring lion, looking for anyone he can devour.

1 Peter 5:8 HCSB

The Lord knows how to deliver the godly out of temptations.

2 Peter 2:9 NKJV

*Put on the whole armor of God,
that you may be able to stand
against the wiles of the devil.*

—

Ephesians 6:11 NKJV

Testimony

But sanctify the Lord God in your hearts, and always be ready to give a defense to everyone who asks you a reason for the hope that is in you.

1 Peter 3:15 HCSB

You are the light of the world. A city that is set on a hill cannot be hidden. Nor do they light a lamp and put it under a basket, but on a lampstand, and it gives light to all who are in the house. Let your light so shine before men, that they may see your good works and glorify your Father in heaven.

Matthew 5:14–16 NKJV

Whatever I tell you in the dark, speak in the light; and what you hear in the ear, preach on the housetops.

Matthew 10:27 NKJV

But as for me, I will never boast about anything except the cross of our Lord Jesus Christ, through whom the world has been crucified to me, and I to the world.

Galatians 6:14 HCSB

And I say to you,
anyone who acknowledges Me
before men, the Son of Man
will also acknowledge him before
the angels of God; but whoever
denies Me before men will be
denied before the angels of God.

—

Luke 12:8-9 HCSB

Thanksgiving

Thanks be to God for His indescribable gift.

2 Corinthians 9:15 HCSB

And let the peace of the Messiah, to which you were also called in one body, control your hearts. Be thankful.

Colossians 3:15 HCSB

It is good to give thanks to the Lord, and to sing praises to Your name, O Most High.

Psalm 92:1 NKJV

Therefore as you have received Christ Jesus the Lord, walk in Him, rooted and built up in Him and established in the faith, just as you were taught, and overflowing with thankfulness.

Colossians 2:6-7 HCSB

Enter into His gates with thanksgiving, and into His courts with praise. Be thankful to Him, and bless His name. For the Lord is good; His mercy is everlasting, and His truth endures to all generations.

Psalm 100:4-5 NKJV

Wisdom

The fear of the Lord is the beginning of wisdom; a good understanding have all those who do His commandments. His praise endures forever.

Psalm 111:10 NKJV

So teach us to number our days, that we may gain a heart of wisdom.

Psalm 90:12 NKJV

A wise man will hear and increase learning, and a man of understanding will attain wise counsel.

Proverbs 1:5 NKJV

Teach me, O Lord, the way of Your statutes, and I shall keep it to the end.

Psalm 119:33 NKJV

Acquire wisdom—how much better it is than gold! And acquire understanding—it is preferable to silver.

Proverbs 16:16 HCSB